A SERIES OF CONDUCT BOOKS

THOEMMES

THOUGHTS ON THE
EDUCATION OF DAUGHTERS

Mary Wollstonecraft

With a new Introduction by
Janet Todd

THOEMMES PRESS

Published in 1995 by
Thoemmes Press
11 Great George Street
Bristol BS1 5RR
England

ISBN 1 85506 381 6

This is a reprint of the 1787 Edition
© Introduction by Janet Todd 1995

Publisher's Note

INTRODUCTION

Thoughts on the Education of Daughters was Mary Wollstonecraft's first published book, a fitting predecessor to her other educational work, her masterpiece *A Vindication of the Rights of Woman*. It told both of the ideas that had shaped her attitude and of the experiences that had impelled her into writing about women and their plight.

Thoughts arose out of a moment in Wollstonecraft's life. After a childhood following around an increasingly drunken and impecunious father, she had escaped, against her family's wishes, into some sort of independence at the age of nineteen by becoming a companion to a Mrs Dawson in Bath. From this rather unsatisfactory post she was, as the eldest daughter, called home to attend her sick mother who died a few months later in April 1782. She then went to live in the family of her close friend Fanny Blood before she was recalled again for a family crisis when her sister Eliza, who had recently married, suffered from depression after the birth of her first child. With foolhardy promptness Wollstonecraft dealt with the situation by removing Eliza from her husband and baby and hiding her until the furore died down.

Now with Fanny Blood and her sister Eliza in tow she set about establishing a school for girls in which all of them, and her other sister Everina, might teach and keep themselves without the aid of fathers or husbands.

For the first school they tried Islington; it was not a success. But their second choice, Newington Green, another one of London's outer suburbs, close to an established Dissenting community, was more fruitful. The school they set up was not exactly flourishing but it did keep the young women for some time.

The most celebrated inhabitant of the Dissenting community was Richard Price, a minister who was also a moral teacher, economist and political polemicist. Wollstonecraft quickly came to know him and even attended his chapel although she remained nominally an Anglican. She was excited by the intellectual milieu in which Dr Price lived. The Dissenting community prided itself on educating its young and continuing education throughout life. Because it itself laboured under political constraints – the Dissenters did not yet have full civil rights and could not, for example, attend the universities – it was sympathetic to other groups that lacked rights or basic freedoms. Consequently she found here a respect for women's intellect that was rare in society at large. Women were not equal: they were not teaching in the Dissenting academies or preaching from the pulpits. But they were arguing and writing about the issues of the day in a way Wollstonecraft had not seen before.

Probably she took time out from her teaching to talk and listen but she was none the less the strongest element among her sisters and Fanny. When Fanny Blood who had long been ailing went to Portugal to marry and subsequently became pregnant, Wollstonecraft felt it her duty to rush to her friend's side. In November 1785 she left her sisters to manage as best they could and sailed off to Portugal. She arrived just in time to see poor Fanny die following childbirth. It was a sore blow to the young woman whose first strong emotional tie outside her family had been to Fanny Blood.

Returning quickly to England – she was back by January of 1786 – she found the school in difficulties and her sisters despairing. There was nothing to do but close the establishment, find places for herself and her sisters as governesses, and prepare for another sort of 'independent' life. The position she found for herself was, on the face of it, a good one: as governess to the daughters of Lord and Lady Kingsborough in Ireland, but she prepared to travel there with considerable misgivings. Before she went she put together the thoughts that had arisen from her months in the school and from her many conversations on the status and role of women with her Dissenting neighbours. She needed to write with speed since she wanted to publish and receive money as soon as possible. With Fanny Blood dead, she believed that the Blood parents had become her responsibility; the money she received was to go for their relief.

She was paid ten pounds and ten shillings for *Thoughts on the Education of Daughters* which was published by Joseph Johnson, a London publisher with close ties to the Dissenting community of Newington Green. If she herself received no pecuniary advantages from her effort, the tie now formed with Johnson was of far greater value in her life. It was with Johnson that she would publish – and have the opportunity to write – her most famous works, *A Vindication of the Rights of Men* and *A Vindication of the Rights of Woman* a few years later.

Thoughts on the Education of Daughters was an appropriate first book since in a way Wollstonecraft would always be an educationist and since it called on the experience of its author. She was a single woman who desperately wanted to make her way in the world as an independent person, depending on no one for money. The money she should have had from her grandfather's will she had seen used by her family and she burned with indignation at the superior education lavished on the eldest son of the family and denied to herself, the eldest daughter. In her chapter entitled 'Unfortunate Situation of Females Fashionably Educated, and Left without a Fortune' she was clearly letting the reader into her own life, for she had had to begin her 'independent' existence as a companion and it might have been Mrs Dawson on whom she was commenting when she wrote, 'Few are the modes of earning a subsistence, and those very humiliating.... [It] is still worse, to live with strangers, who are so intolerably tyrannical that none of their own relations can bear to live with them.' She could also say in life as she did in her work, that 'nothing...calls forth the faculties so much as being obliged to struggle with the world'. Her life over the last few years since she had left home for Bath had been little but an obligation to struggle.

If some of her remarks drew on her past experience, others were unhappily prescient. In her chapter on 'Love' she managed to foreshadow her future unhappy love affair with the American merchant Gilbert Imlay when she wrote: 'People of sense and reflection are most apt to have violent and constant passions, and to be preyed on by them.... Perhaps a delicate mind is not susceptible of a greater degree of misery...than what must arise from the consciousness of loving a person whom their reason does not approve.'

Also clear from the book was her experience with the few girls who had come to the school in Newington

Green. When she, Fanny Blood and her sisters ran their day school, she had evidently been less than enthralled with her teaching. Girls of school age were not pliable, it seems, and she needed to consider how they had got into their inflexible way and what might be done about it. It became clear to her – no doubt also from her own experience as a daughter of an unsatisfactory and neglectful mother – that parents were not *naturally* parents.

It was thus to mothers that she primarily addressed her book. Mothers must somehow change so that they could decently teach their daughters who would in turn give proper training themselves when they became mothers. Although she herself was deeply emotional and indeed prided herself on her sensibility, her experience with adolescent girls had made her value the idea of rational motherhood. It was clear that home life had a greater effect on girls than school learning and that the most basic form of development was imitation. Thus it was parents rather than teachers or governesses who had the greatest influence on young girls. A woman to be a proper and useful mother must know herself and analyse her character.

For women who did not marry there should be some roles outside the family and some preparation for them, though Wollstonecraft could not yet look much beyond her own experience. Accomplishments were fine for the cosseted woman and they might also help the unfortunately independent one likewise. But they were not to be relied on and something more was needed to bolster the unfamilial woman in adversity. This something was reason: with the optimism of the new rationalist, she accepted that the exercise of reason would lead to virtuous conduct. But, however mitigated by reason and virtue, women's lot did not appear a happy one: what the book mainly reveals was the very narrow range of options open to someone like herself, a reasonably educated middle class woman. It was both realistic and defensive therefore to insist, as she did, that for women the primary role would remain motherhood.

Later Wollstonecraft's rationalism as well as her emotional experience would undermine her religious piety. But in *Thoughts* her conventional Anglicanism coexisted with reason and she urged women to use reason to prepare for a better afterlife. The miseries of earthly existence, which she graphically portrayed in a woman's unnurtured or unfamilial existence, might be combated with the fortitude of a rational mind but they would only be compensated for by heavenly happiness. The knowledge to be gained through education was moral as well as mental, then, religious as well as rational.

Because of this pious emphasis Wollstonecraft noted but did not attack the social subordination of women and the domestic roles to which they were mostly confined. This situation was unfortunate but it remained divinely sanctioned. It might be mitigated by self-analysis and development of the mind but not essentially changed. Society demanded many compromises and capitulations: a woman who had trained her mind would be able to analyse these and trust in her own judgement both for herself and for her young daughter.

Although there was a certainty that environment influences character, Wollstonecraft still held to a sense of fate and divine disposition. She wanted a girl's lot to be modified as much as possible by the existence of a rational mother. Otherwise she accepted it much as it was and counselled a wise passivity in the face of inevitable obstacles. It was the sense of resignation that made *Thoughts* a conservative document in many ways, not unlike the educational work of any commonsensical and conservative woman writer of the day such as Hannah More.

Her treatment of servants also allied Wollstonecraft with conservative conduct book writers and differed markedly from her later sympathy. Where in *Letters Written in Sweden* she would come to feel compassion for the lot of women servants, labouring under a double disadvantage of sex and class, here she firmly took the view of the upper orders, that servants were a sort of children and that they needed controlling as much as children. They were usually a disastrous influence on the daughters of the families in which they worked, not because of the class consciousness they instilled but because of their vulgarity, which necessarily rubbed off on the children of higher rank and moderated the advantages of their higher status.

Since she was advocating rational motherhood Wollstonecraft criticized actual mothers for their self-indulgence and lack of proper restraint. She did not indulge herself in those sorts of effusions about motherhood that had become so common in senti-mental literature by women. In these the very word 'mother', often capitalized, opened floodgates of emotion, as it did, for example, in the vindications of the sentimental novelist Mrs Gunning when she desired to go before the public as an exemplary mother of a virtuous daughter. Because Wollstonecraft took a more rational stance than Mrs Gunning and, indeed, a more rational one than she herself would take in her next far more self-indulgent book *Mary, A Fiction*, in *Thoughts* she accepted the reasonable but unfashionable principle that maternal bonding with the infant came as 'much from habit as instinct'. Hence in place of the amazing scenes in sentimental literature where a grown daughter and an estranged mother immediately recognize each other and fall into each other's arms, she insisted that the mother-daughter bond was made through caring, through breast-feeding and proper attention to education.

If experience fuelled the book, it was also very derivative in its opinions. Wollstonecraft was genuinely excited about the pedagogical ideas she was meeting among her friends in Newington Green for they suggested, despite their inherent piety, a possibility of change which she herself had not yet quite taken on board. In general her ideas consisted of a sort of developmental psychology based on Locke and David Hartley: she may even have read Locke's influential treatise *Some Thoughts Concerning Education* (1690) which might have suggested her title to her, although his notions were by now present in the culture and popularly presented. Locke had stressed the importance of early environment and the need to bring out the capabilities of small children, indicating that education was more of a process than a product. Wollstonecraft may have come close to Locke's ideas through her friend Sarah Burgh, the widow of James Burgh who had been concerned with education and written on the subject in the Lockean mode.

If she derived from male writers on the subject of education, sadly she showed no evidence of having read earlier women such as Bathsua Makin and Mary Astell writing in the late seventeenth and early eighteenth centuries. Before the triumph of sentimental propaganda and the growth in middle-class desire for an education in accomplishments for their daughters, these two women had put forward ideas for a rational training for women that fitted them for a life of intellectual rigor. Astell in particular required an examination of one's experience and a constant interrogation of one's ideas that were far from the passive acceptance of rules into which most girls were 'educated'.

Although it is miles away from the picture of the contingent woman drawn by Rousseau in his *Emile*, Wollstonecraft's emphasis in her *Thoughts* on passivity and piety makes her nearer than she would later be to the men she opposed in *A Vindication of the Rights of Woman*; there she deplored the patronizing attitude of John Fordyce and James Gregory who urged girls forward as good daughters preparing to be good wives. But even in *Thoughts* she did not follow Fordyce into his aestheticized piety or condone the pictures of girls promoting their retiring graces into almost seductive arts. She was not as assertive and as sure as she would become when she penned *A Vindication of the Rights of Woman* when she was fully aware of the pernicious influence of the propaganda that insisted on women's timidity and sensitivity as their chief attractions, but already she was insisting on women's capacity, even duty, to reason. What she had not realized because she had not experienced it, was that there were other roles open to women besides wife and mother or despised governess and companion.

Thoughts on Education is unsatisfactory in many ways. Although vigorously promoting education Wollstonecraft failed to say much about what exactly girls should be taught. If she implied the Lockean idea that the child was to be trained as rational and autonomous and the girl should try as much as was possible to become equivalent of the rational entrepreneurial boy, she yet avoided surrounding the idea with any sense that social change was wanted; the girl must be rigorously trained but, if her training was at odds with the role she was to play in adult life, Wollstonecraft had nothing to say on how she might soothe her dilemma.

Thoughts on the Education of Daughters is aptly named. It gives an appearance of being 'thoughts' rather than a single and integrated argument. The sections are like separate pieces brought together through the personality of the author. In this respect it is prophetic, since all Wollstonecraft's major works will exude this strong sense of her personality. If *Thoughts* is not absolutely prophetic of *A Vindication of the Rights of Woman* in content, it does mark the beginning of Wollstonecraft as a professional writer: it was the confidence that such publication gave her that allowed her to compose her great work when the moment and she herself were both right.

Janet Todd
Norwich, 1995

THOUGHTS

ON THE

EDUCATION

OF

DAUGHTERS:

WITH

REFLECTIONS ON FEMALE CONDUCT,

IN

The more important DUTIES of LIFE.

By MARY WOLLSTONECRAFT.

LONDON:

PRINTED FOR J. JOHNSON, N°72, ST. PAUL'S
CHURCH-YARD.

M DCC LXXXVII.

PREFACE.

IN the following pages I have endeavoured to point out some important things with respect to female education. It is true, many treatises have been already written; yet it occurred to me, that much still remained to be said. I shall not swell these sheets by writing apologies for my attempt. I am afraid, indeed, the reflections will, by some, be thought too grave; but I could not make them less so without writing af-

fectedly;

fectedly; yet, though they may be
infipid to the gay, others may not
think them fo; and if they fhould
prove ufeful to one fellow-creature, and beguile any hours, which
forrow has made heavy, I fhall
think I have not been employed
in vain.

THOUGHTS

THOUGHTS

ON THE

EDUCATION

OF

DAUGHTERS.

The NURSERY.

A S I conceive it to be the duty of
every rational creature to attend to its offspring, I am forry to obferve, that reafon and duty together
have not fo powerful an influence over

B human

human conduct, as inſtinct has in the brute creation. Indolence, and a thoughtleſs diſregard of every thing, except the preſent indulgence, make many mothers, who may have momentary ſtarts of tenderneſs, neglect their children. They follow a pleaſing impulſe, and never reflect that reaſon ſhould cultivate and govern thoſe inſtincts which are implanted in us to render the path of duty pleaſant—for if they are not governed they will run wild; and ſtrengthen the paſſions which are ever endeavouring to obtain dominion—I mean vanity and ſelf-love.

The

The firft thing to be attended to, is laying the foundation of a good conftitution. The mother (if there are not very weighty reafons to prevent her) ought to fuckle her children. Her milk is their proper nutriment, and for fome time is quite fufficient. Were a regular mode of fuckling a-dopted, it would be far from being a laborious tafk. Children, who are left to the care of ignorant nurfes, have their ftomachs overloaded with impro-per food, which turns acid, and renders them very uncomfortable. We fhould be particularly careful to guard them in their infant ftate from bodily pain; as their minds can then afford them no

amufe-

amufement to alleviate it. The firft
years of a child's life are frequently
made miferable through negligence or
ignorance. Their complaints are moftly in their ftomach or bowels; and
thefe complaints generally arife from
the quality and quantity of their food.

The fuckling of a child alfo excites
the warmeft glow of tendernefs—Its
dependant, helplefs ftate produces an
affection, which may properly be termed maternal. I have even felt it, when
I have feen a mother perform that
office; and am of opinion, that maternal tendernefs arifes quite as much
from habit as inftinct. It is poffible, I

m

am convinced, to acquire the affection
of a parent for an adopted child; it is
neceffary, therefore, for a mother to
perform the office of one, in order to
produce in herfelf a rational affection
for her offspring.

Children very early contract the
manners of thofe about them. It is
eafy to diftinguifh the child of a well-
bred perfon, if it is not left entirely to
the nurfe's care. Thefe women are
of courfe ignorant, and to keep a child
quiet for the moment, they humour
all its little caprices. Very foon does
it begin to be perverfe, and eager to
be gratified in every thing. The ufual

mode

mode of acting is complying with the
humours fometimes, and contradicting
them at others—juft according to the
dictates of an uncorrected temper.
This the infant finds out earlier than
can be imagined, and it gives rife to
an affection devoid of refpect. Uni-
formity of conduct is the only feafible
method of creating both. An inflexible adherence to any rule that has
been laid down makes children comfortable, and faves the mother and
nurfe much trouble, as they will not
often conteft, if they have not once
conquered. They will, I am fure,
love and refpect a perfon who treats
them properly, if fome one elfe does

not

not indifcreetly indulge them. I once heard a judicious father fay, " He would treat his child as he would his horfe : firft convince it he was its maiter, and then its friend." But yet a rigid ftyle of behaviour is by no means to be adopted; on the contrary, I wifh to remark, that it is only in the years of childhood that the happinefs of a human being depends entirely on others—and to embitter thofe years by needlefs reftraint is cruel. To conciliate affection, affection muft be fhown, and little proofs of it ought always to be given—let them not appear weakneffes, and they will fink deep into the young mind, and call

forth

forth its moſt amiable propenſities,. The turbulent paſſions may be kept down till reaſon begins to dawn.

In the nurſery too, they are taught to ſpeak ; and there they not only hear nonſenſe, but that nonſenſe retailed out in ſuch ſilly, affected tones as muſt diſguſt ;—yet theſe are the tones which the child firſt imitates, and its inno-cent playful manner renders them tolerable, if not pleaſing ; but after-wards they are not eaſily got the better of—nay, many women always retain the pretty prattle of the nurſery, and do not forget to liſp, when they have learnt to languiſh.

Children

Children are taught revenge and lies in their very cradles. If they fall down, or ſtrike their heads againſt any thing, to quiet them they are bid return the injury, and their little hands held out to do it. When they cry, or are troubleſome, the cat or dog is chaſtiſed, or ſome bugbear called to take them away; which only terrifies them at firſt, for they ſoon find out that the nurſe means nothing by theſe dreadful threatenings. Indeed, ſo well do they diſcover the fallacy, that I have ſeen little creatures, who could ſcarcely ſpeak, play over the ſame tricks with their doll or the cat.

How,

How, then, when the mind comes under difcipline, can precepts of truth be inforced, when the firft examples they have had would lead them to practife the contrary?

MORAL

MORAL DISCIPLINE.

IT has been afferted, " That no being, merely human, could properly
educate a child." I entirely coincide
with this author; but though perfection cannot be attained, and unfore-
feen events will ever govern human
conduct, yet ftill it is our duty to lay
down fome rule to regulate our actions by, and to adhere to it, as confift-
ently as our infirmities will permit.
To be able to follow Mr. Locke's fyf-
tem (and this may be faid of almoft
all treatifes on education) the parents
muft have fubdued their own paffions,
which

which is not often the cafe in any confiderable degree..

The marriage ftate is too often a
ftate of difcord; it does not always
happen that both parents are rational,
and the weakeft have it in their power
to do moft mifchief.

How then are the tender minds
of children to be cultivated?——
Mamma is only anxious that they
fhould love her beft, and perhaps
takes pains to fow thofe feeds,
which have produced fuch luxuriant
weeds in her own mind. Or, what ftill
more frequently occurs, the children
are at firft made play-things of, and
when

when their tempers have been fpoiled by indifcreet indulgence, they become troublefome, and are moftly left with fervants; the firft notions they imbibe, therefore, are mean and vulgar. They are taught cunning, the wifdom of that clafs of people, and a love of truth, the foundation of virtue, is foon obliterated from their minds. It is, in my opinion, a well-proved fact, that principles of truth are innate. Without reafoning we affent to many truths; we feel their force, and artful fophiftry can only blunt thofe feelings which nature has implanted in us as inftinctive guards to virtue. Diffimulation and cunning will foon drive all other

good

good qualities before them, and deprive the mind of that beautiful simplicity, which can never be too much cherished.

Indeed it is of the utmost confequence to make a child artlefs, or to fpeak with more propriety, not to teach them to be otherwife; and in order to do fo we muft keep them out of the way of bad examples. Art is almoft always practifed by fervants, and the fame methods which children obferve them to ufe, to fhield themfelves from blame, they will adopt— and cunning is fo nearly allied to falfehood, that it will infallibly lead to it—

I   or

or some foolish prevaricating subter-
fuge will occur, to silence any re-
proaches of the mind which may arise,
if an attention to truth has been inculcated.

Another cause or source of art is in-
judicious correction. Accidents or
giddy tricks are too frequently pu-
nished, and if children can conceal
these, they will, to avoid chastisement.
Restrain them, therefore, but never
correct them without a very sufficient
cause ; such as a violation of truth,
cruelty to animals, inferiors, or those
kind of follies which lead to vice.

Children

Children fhould be permitted to enter into converfation; but it requires great difcernment to find out fuch fubjects as will gradually improve them. Animals are the firft objects which catch their attention; and I think little ftories about them would not only amufe but inftruct at the fame time, and have the beft effect in forming the temper and cultivating the good difpofitions of the heart. There are many little books which have this tendency. One in particular I recollect: The Perambulations of a Moufe. I cannot here help mentioning a book of hymns, in meafured profe, written by the ingenious author

of

of many other proper leffons for children. Thefe hymns, I imagine, would
contribute to fill the heart with religious fentiments and affections; and,
if I may be allowed the expreffion,
make the Deity obvious to the fenfes.
The underftanding, however, fhould
not be overloaded any more than the
ftomach. Intellectual improvements,
like the growth and formation of the
body, muft be gradual—yet there is no
reafon why the mind fhould lie fallow,
while its " frail tenement" is imperceptibly fitting itfelf for a more reafonable inhabitant. It will not lie fallow; promifcuous feeds will be fown
by accident, and they will fhoot up

C   with

with the wheat, and perhaps never be eradicated.

Whenever a child afks a queftion, it fhould always have a reafonable anfwer given it. Its little paffions fhould be engaged. They are moftly fond of ftories, and proper ones would improve them even while they are amufed. Inftead of thefe, their heads are filled with improbable tales, and fuperftitious accounts of invifible beings, which breed ftrange prejudices and vain fears in their minds.

The lifp of the nurfery is confirmed, and vulgar phrafes are acquired; which children, if poffible, fhould never hear.

3   To

To be able to exprefs the thoughts with facility and propriety, is of great con-fequence in life, and if children were never led aftray in this particular, it would prevent much trouble.

The riot too of the kitchen, or any other place where children are left only with fervants, makes the decent reftraint of the parlour irkfome. A girl, who has vivacity, foon grows a romp; and if there are male fervants, they go out a walking with them, and will frequently take little freedoms with Mifs, the bearing with which gives a forwardnefs to her air, and makes her pert. The becoming mo-

defty,

defty, which being accuftomed to converfe with fuperiors, will give a girl,
is entirely done away.   I muft own,
I am quite charmed when I fee a fweet
young creature, fhrinking as it were
from obfervation, and liftening rather
than talking.   It is poffible a girl may
have this manner without having a very
good underftanding.   If it fhould be
fo, this diffidence prevents her from
being troublefome.

It is the duty of a parent to preferve
a child from receiving wrong impref-
fions.—As to prejudices, the firft notions we have deferve that name ; for
it is not till we begin to waver in our
opinions,

opinions, that we exert our reason to examine them—and then, if they are received, they may be called our own.

The first things, then, that children ought to be encouraged to observe, are a strict adherence to truth; a proper submission to superiors; and condescension to inferiors. These are the main articles; but there are many others, which compared to them are trivial, and yet are of importance. It is not pleasing to see a child full of bows and grimaces; yet they need not be suffered to be rude. They should be employed, and such fables and tales may be culled out for them as would

C 3 excite

excite their curiofity.   A tafte for the beauties of nature fhould be very early cultivated : many things, with refpect to the vegetable and animal world, may be explained in an amufing way ; and this is an innocent fource of plea- fure within every one's reach.

Above all, try to teach them to combine their ideas.   It is of more ufe than can be conceived, for a child to learn to compare things that are fimi- lar in fome refpects, and different in others.   I wifh them to be taught to think—thinking, indeed, is a fevere exercife, and exercife of either mind or body will not at firft be entered on, but

with

with a view to pleafure. Not that I
would have them make long reflections; for when they do not arife
from experience, they are moftly
abfurd.

EXTERIOR ACCOMPLISH-
MENTS.

UNDER this head may be ranked all thofe accomplifhments which merely render the perfon attractive; and thofe half-learnt ones which do not improve the mind. " A little learning of any kind is a dangerous thing ;" and fo far from making a perfon pleafing, it has the contrary effect.

Parents have moftly fome weighty weighty bufinefs in hand, which they make a pretext to themfelves for neglecting the arduous tafk of educating their child en ; they are therefore fent

8   to

to fchool, and the allowance for them is fo low, that the perfon who under-takes the charge muft have more than fhe can poffibly attend to; of courfe, the mechanical parts of education can only be obferved. I have known chil-dren who could repeat things in the order they learnt them, that were quite at a lofs when put out of the beaten track. If the underftanding is not ex-ercifed, the memory will be employed to little purpofe.

Girls learn fomething of mufic, drawing, and geography; but they do not know enough to engage their atten-tion, and render it an employment of the mind. If they can play over a few

tunes

tunes to their acquaintance, and have a drawing or two (half done by the mafter) to hang up in their rooms, they imagine themfelves artifts for the reft of their lives. It is not the being able to execute a trifling landfcape, or any thing of the kind, that is of confequence—Thefe are at beft but trifles, and the foolifh, indifcriminate praifes which are be-ftowed on them only produce vanity. But what is really of no importance, when confidered in this light, becomes of the utmoft, when a girl has a fond-nefs for the art, and a defire of excel-lence. Whatever tends to make a perfon in fome meafure independent

of

of the senses, is a prop to virtue. A-
musing employments must first occupy
the mind; and as an attention to moral duties leads to piety, so whoever
weighs one subject will turn to others,
and new ideas will rush into the mind.
The faculties will be exercised, and
not suffered to sleep, which will give a
variety to the character.

Dancing and elegance of manners
are very pleasing, if too great a stress
is not laid on them. These acquire-
ments catch the senses, and open the
way to the heart; but unsupported by
solid good qualities, their reign is short.

The lively thoughtlessness of youth
makes every young creature agreeable

for

for the time; but when thofe years
are flown, and fenfe is not fubftituted
in the ftead of vivacity, the follies of
youth are acted over, and they never
confider, that the things which pleafe
in their proper feafon, difguft out of it.
It is very abfurd to fee a woman,
whofe brow time has marked with
wrinkles, aping the manners of a girl
in her teens.

I do not think it foreign to the prefent fubject to mention the trifling converfations women are moftly fond of.
In general, they are prone to ridicule.
As they lay the greateft ftrefs on manners, the moft refpectable characters
will

will not efcape its lafh, if deficient in
this article. Ridicule has been, with
fome people, the boafted teft of truth
—if fo, our fex ought to make won-
derful improvements; but I am apt to
think, they often exert this talent till
they lofe all perception of it themfelves.
Affectation, and not ignorance, is the
fair game for ridicule; and even affectation fome good-natured perfons
will fpare. We fhould never give pain
without a defign to amend.

Exterior accomplifhments are not to
be defpifed, if the acquiring of them
does not fatisfy the poffeffors, and prevent their cultivating the more important ones.

ARTI-

ARTIFICIAL MANNERS.

IT may be thought, that artificial manners and exterior accomplifh-ments are much the fame.; but I think the former take a far wider range, and are materially different. The one arifes from affectation, and the other feems only an error in judgment.

The emotions of the mind often appear confpicuous in the countenance and manner. Thefe emotions, when they arife from fenfibility and virtue, are inexpreffibly pleafing. But it is eafier to copy the caft of countenance, than to cultivate the virtues which animate and improve it.

How

How many people are like whitened fepulchres, and careful only about appearances! yet if we are too anxious to gain the approbation of the world, we muft often forfeit our own.

How bewitching is that humble softnefs of manners which humility gives birth to, and how faint are the imitations of affectation! That gentlenefs of behaviour, which makes us courteous to all, and that benevolence, which makes us loth to offend any, and ftudious to pleafe every creature, is fometimes copied by the polite; but how aukward is the copy! The warmeft profeffions of regard are prof-

tituted

tituted on all occafions. No diftinc-
tions are made, and the efteem which
is only due to merit, appears to be
lavifhed on all—Nay, affection is affected; at leaft, the language is bor-
rowed, when there is no glow of it in
the heart. Civility is due to all, but
regard or admiration fhould never be
expreffed when it is not felt.

As humility gives the moft pleafing
caft to the countenance, fo from fin-
cerity arifes that artleffnefs of manners
which is fo engaging. She who fuffers herfelf to be feen as fhe really is,
can never be thought affected. She
is not folicitous to act a part; her endeavour

deavour is not to hide; but correct
her failings, and her face has of courſe
that beauty, which an attention to the
mind only gives. I never knew a perſon really ugly, who was not fooliſh
or vicious; and I have ſeen the moſt
beautiful features deformed by paſſion
and vice. It is true, regular features
ſtrike at firſt; but it is a well ordered
mind which occaſions thoſe turns of
expreſſion in the countenance, which
make a laſting impreſſion.

Feeling is ridiculous when affected;
and even when felt, ought not to be
diſplayed. It will appear if genuine;
but when puſhed forward to notice, it
is obvious vanity has rivalled ſorrow,

and that the prettinefs of the thing is thought of. Let the manners arife from the mind, and let there be no difguife for the genuine emotions of the heart.

Things merely ornamental are foon difregarded, and difregard can fcarcely be borne when there is no internal fupport.

To have in this uncertain world fome ftay, which cannot be undermined, is of the utmoft confequence; and this ftay it is, which gives that dignity to the manners, which fhews that a perfon does not depend on mere human applaufe for comfort and fatisfaction.

DRESS.

D R E S S.

MANY able pens have dwelt on the peculiar foibles of our fex. We have been equally defired to avoid the two extremes in drefs, and the neceffity of cleanlinefs has been infifted on, " As from the body's purity the mind receives a fympathetic aid."

By far too much of a girl's time is taken up in drefs. This is an exterior accomplifhment; but I chofe to confider it by itfelf. The body hides the mind, and it is, in its turn, obfcured by the drapery. I hate to fee the frame of a picture fo glaring, as to

catch

catch the eye and divide the attention. Drefs ought to adorn the perfon, and not rival it. It may be fimple, elegant, and becoming, without being expenfive; and ridiculous fafhions difregarded, while fingularity is avoided. The beauty of drefs (I fhall raife aftonifhment by faying fo) is its not being confpicuous one way or the other; when it neither diftorts, or hides the human form by unnatural protuberances. If ornaments are much ftudied, a confcioufnefs of being well dreffed will appear in the face—and furely this mean pride does not give much fublimity to it.

" Out

" Out of the abundance of the heart the mouth fpeaketh." And how much converfation does drefs furnifh, which furely cannot be very improving or entertaining.

It gives rife to envy, and contefts for trifling fuperiority, which do not render a woman very refpectable to the other fex.

Arts are ufed to obtain money; and much is fquandered away, which if faved for charitable purpofes, might alleviate the diftrefs of many poor families, and foften the heart of the girl who entered into fuch fcenes of woe.

D 3 In

In the article of dreſs may be included the whole tribe of beauty-
waſhes, coſmetics, Olympian dew, ori-
ental herbs, liquid bloom, and the
paint which enlivened Ninon's face,
and bid defiance to time. Theſe numerous and eſſential articles are ad-
vertiſed in ſo ridiculous a ſtyle, that
the rapid ſale of them is a very ſevere
reflection on the underſtanding of thoſe
females who encourage it. The dew
and herbs, I imagine, are very harm-
leſs, but I do not know whether the
ſame may be ſaid of the paint. White
is certainly very prejudicial to the
health, and never can be made to re-
ſemble nature. The red, too, takes

off from the expreſſion of the countenance, and the beautiful glow which
modeſty, affeſtion, or any other emotion of the mind, gives, can never be
ſeen. It is not " a mind-illumined
face." " The body does not charm,
becauſe the mind is ſeen," but juſt the
contrary; and if caught by it a man
marries a woman thus diſguiſed, he
may chance not to be ſatisfied with her
real perſon. A made-up face may
ſtrike viſitors, but will certainly diſguſt
domeſtic friends. And one obvious
inference is drawn, truth is not expeſt-
ed to govern the inhabitant of ſo artificial a form. The falſe life with which
rouge animates the eyes, is not of the

D 4 moſt

moft delicate kind ; nor does a wo--
man's dreffing herfelf in a way to at-
tract languifhing glances, give us the
moft advantageous opinion of the purity of her mind.

I forgot to mention powder among
the deceptions. It is a pity that it fhould
be fo generally worn. The moft beautiful ornament of the features is difguif-
ed, and the fhade it would give to the
countenance entirely loft. The color
of every perfon's. hair generally fuits
the complexion, and is calculated to
fet it off. What abfurdity then do
they run into, who ufe red, blue, and
yellow powder!—And what a falfe
tafte does it exhibit!

                                    The

The quantity of pomatum is often difgufting. We laugh at the Hottentots, and in fome things adopt their cuftoms.

Simplicity of Drefs, and unaffected manners, fhould go together. They demand refpect, and will be admired by people of tafte, even when love is out of the queftion.

THE

The FINE ARTS.

MUSIC and painting, and many other ingenious arts, are now brought to great perfection, and afford the moft rational and delicate pleafure.

It is eafy to find out if a young perfon has a tafte for them. If they have, do not fuffer it to lie dormant. Heaven kindly beftowed it, and a great bleffing it is ; but, like all other bleffings, may be perverted: yet the intrinfic value is not leffened by the perverfion. Should nature have been a niggard to them in this refpect, perfuade

them

them to be filent, and not feign rap-
tures they do not feel; for nothing
can be more ridiculous.

In mufic I prefer exprefhon to execution. The fimple melody of fome
artlefs airs has often foothed my mind,
when it has been harraffed by care;
and I have been raifed from the very
depths of forrow, by the fublime harmony of fome of Handel's compofi-
tions. I have been lifted above this
little fcene of grief and care, and mufed
on Him, from whom all bounty flows.

A perfon muft have fenfe, tafte, and
fenfibility, to render their mufic interefting.

resting. The nimble dance of the fingers may raise wonder, but not delight.

As to drawing, those cannot be really charmed by it, who do not observe the beauties of nature, and even admire them.

If a person is fond of tracing the effects of the passions, and marking the appearances they give to the countenance, they will be glad to see characters displayed on canvas, and enter into the spirit of them; but if by them the book of nature has not been read, their admiration is childish.

Works

Works of fancy are very amuſing, if a girl has a lively fancy; but if ſhe makes others do the greateſt part of them, and only wiſhes for the credit of doing them, do not encourage her.

Writing may be termed a fine art; and, I am ſure, it is a very uſeful one. The ſtyle in particular deſerves atten-tion. Young people are very apt to ſubſtitute words for ſentiments, and clothe mean thoughts in pompous dic-tion. Induſtry and time are neceſſary to cure this, and will often do it. Children ſhould be led into correſpon-dences, and methods adopted to make them write down their ſentiments, and

they

they fhould be prevailed on to relate the ftories they have read in their own words. Writing well is of great confequence in life as to our temporal intereft, and of ftill more to the mind; as it teaches a perfon to arrange their thoughts, and digeft them. Befides, it forms the only true bafis of rational and elegant converfation.

Reading, and fuch arts as have been already mentioned, would fill up the time, and prevent a young perfon's being loft in diffipation, which enervates the mind, and often leads to improper connections. When habits are fixed, and a character in fome meafure formed, the entering into the

busy

buſy world, ſo far from being dangerous, is uſeful. Knowledge will imperceptibly be acquired, and the taſte improved, if admiration is not more ſought for than improvement. For thoſe ſeldom make obſervation who are full of themſelves.

READING.

READING.

IT is an old, but a very true obfervation, that the human mind muft
ever be employed. A relifh for reading, or any of the fine arts, fhould be
cultivated very early in life; and thofe
who reflect can tell, of what importance it is for the mind to have fome re-
fource in itfelf, and not to be entirely
dependant on the fenfes for employment and amufement. If it unfortunately is fo, it muft fubmit to meannefs, and often to vice, in order to
gratify them. The wifeft and beft are
too much under their influence; and
the endeavouring to conquer them,

when

when reafon and virtue will not give their fanction, conftitutes great part of the warfare of life. What fupport, then, have they who are all fenfes, and who are full of fchemes, which terminate in temporal objects?

Reading is the moft rational employment, if people feek food for the underftanding, and do not rea merely to remember words; or with a view to quote celebrated authors, and retail fentiments they do not underftand or feel. Judicious books enlarge the mind and improve the heart, though fome, by them, " are made coxcombs " whom nature meant for fools."

E   Thofe

Thofe productions which give a wrong account of the human paffions, and the various accidents of life, ought not to be read before the judgment is formed, or at leaft exercifed. Such accounts are one great caufe of the affectation of young women. Senfibility is defcribed and praifed, and the effects of it reprefented in a way fo different from nature, that thofe who imitate it muft make themfelves very ridiculous. A falfe tafte is acquired, and fenfible books appear dull and infipid after thofe fuperficial performances, which obtain their full end if they can keep the mind in a continual ferment. Gallantry is made the only interefting

fubject

fubject with the novelift; reading,
therefore, will often co-operate to make
his fair admirers infignificant.

I do not mean to recommend books
of an abftracted or grave caft. There
are in our language many, in which
inftruction and amufement are blend-
ed; the Adventurer is of this kind.
I mention this book on account of
its beautiful allegories and affect-
ing tales, and fimilar ones may eafily
be felected. Reafon ftrikes moft
forcibly when illuftrated by the bril-
liancy of fancy. The fentiments
which are fcattered may be obferved,
and when they are relifhed, and the

E 2   mind

mind fet to work, it may be allowed to chufe books for itfelf, for every thing will then inftruct.

I would have every one try to form an opinion of an author themfelves, though modefty may reftrain them from mentioning it. Many are fo anxious to have the reputation of tafte, that they only praife the authors whofe merit is indifputable. I am fick of hearing of the fublimity of Milton, the elegance and harmony of Pope, and the original, untaught genius of Shake-fpear. Thefe curfory remarks are made by fome who know nothing of nature, and could not enter into the

fpirit

2

spirit of those authors, or understand
them.

A florid style mostly passes with the
ignorant for fine writing; many sen-
tences are admired that have no mean-
ing in them, though they contain
" words of thundering found," and
others that have nothing to recommend them but sweet and musical
terminations.

Books of theology are not calculated
for young persons; religion is best
taught by example. The Bible should
be read with particular respect, and
they should not be taught reading by

E 3   so

fo facred a book; left they might confider that as a tafk, which ought to be
a fource of the moft exalted fatisfaction.

It may be obferved, that I recommend the mind's being put into a proper train, and then left to itfelf.   Fixed
rules cannot be given, it muft depend
on the nature and ftrength of the underftanding; and thofe who obferve
it can beft tell what kind of cultiva-
tion will improve it.   The mind is not,
cannot be created by the teacher,
though it may be cultivated, and its
real powers found out.

The active fpirits of youth may
make time glide away without intel-
leЄtual

lectual enjoyments ; but when the novelty of the scene is worn off, the want
of them will be felt, and nothing else
can fill up the void. The mind is
confined to the body, and muft fink
into fenfuality ; for it has nothing to
do but to provide for it, " how it fhall
eat and drink, and wherewithal it fhall
be clothed."

All kinds of refinement have been
found fault with for increafing our
cares and forrows ; yet furely the
contrary effect alfo arifes from them.
Tafte and thought open many fources
of pleafure, which do not depend on
fortune.

4   No

No employment of the mind is a sufficient excuse for neglecting domestic duties, and I cannot conceive that they are incompatible. A woman may fit herself to be the companion and friend of a man of sense, and yet know how to take care of his family.

BOARD-

BOARDING-SCHOOLS.

IF a mother has leifure and good fenfe, and more than one daughter, I think fhe could beft educate them herfelf; but as many family reafons render it neceffary fometimes to fend them from home, boarding-fchools are fixed on. I muft own it is my opinion, that the manners are too much attended to in all fchools; and in the nature of things it cannot be otherwife, as the reputation of the houfe depends upon it, and moft people can judge of them. The temper is neglected, the fame leffons are taught to all, and fome get a fmatter-

ing

ing of things they have not capacity ever to underſtand; few things are learnt thoroughly, but many follies contracted, and an immoderate fondneſs for dreſs among the reſt.

To prepare a woman to fulfil the important duties of a wife and mother, are certainly the objects that ſhould be in view during the early period of life; yet accompliſhments are moſt thought of, and they, and all-powerful beauty, generally gain the heart; and as the keeping of it is not conſidered of until it is loſt, they are deemed of the moſt conſequence. A ſenſible governeſs cannot attend to the

minds

minds of the number fhe is obliged to
have. She may have been many years
ftruggling to get eftablifhed, and when
fortune fmiles, does not chufe to lofe
the opportunity of providing for old
age; therefore continues to enlarge her
fchool, with a view to accumulate a
competency for that purpofe. Domeftic concerns cannot poffibly be
made a part of their employment, or
proper converfations often entered on.
Improper books will by ftealth be in-
troduced, and the bad example of
one or two vicious children, in the
play-hours, infect a number. Their
gratitude and tendernefs are not called
forth in the way they might be by
maternal

maternal affection. Many miseries does
a girl of a mild disposition suffer, which
a tender parent could guard her from.
I shall not contest about the graces,
but the virtues are best learnt at home,
if a mother will give up her time and
thoughts to the task; but if she cannot, they should be sent to school; for
people who do not manage their children well, and have not large fortunes,
must leave them often with servants,
where they are in danger of still greater
corruptions.

THE

The TEMPER.

THE forming of the temper ought
to be the continual thought, and
the firſt taſk of a parent or teacher.
For to ſpeak moderately, half the mi-
ſeries of life ariſe from peeviſhneſs,
or a tyrannical domineering temper.
The tender, who are ſo by nature, or
thoſe whom religion has moulded with
ſo heavenly a diſpoſition, give way for
the ſake of peace—yet ſtill this giving
way undermines their domeſtic comfort, and ſtops the current of affection;
they labor for patience, and labor
is ever painful.

The

The governing of our temper is truly the bufinefs of our whole lives; but furely it would very much affift us if we were early put into the right road. As it is, when reafon gains fome ftrength, fhe has mountains of rubbifh to remove, or perhaps exerts all her powers to juftify the errors of folly and paffion, rather than root them out.

A conftant attention to the management of the temper produces gentlenefs and humility, and is practifed on all occafions, as it is not done " to be feen of men." This meek fpirit arifes from good fenfe and refolution, and fhould not be confounded with indolence

lence and timidity; weaknesses of mind,
which often pass for good nature. She
who submits, without conviction, to a
parent or husband, will as unreason-
ably tyrannise over her servants; for
slavish fear and tyranny go together.
Resentment, indeed, may and will be
felt occasionally by the best of human
beings; yet humility will soon conquer it, and convert scorn and contempt into pity, and drive out that
hasty pride which is always guarding
Self from insult; which takes fire on the
most trivial occasions, and which will not
admit of a superior, or even an equal.
With such a temper is often joined
that bashful aukwardness which arises

from

from ignorance, and is frequently termed diffidence; but which does not, in
my opinion, deferve fuch a diftinction.
True humility is not innate, but like
every other good quality muft be cultivated. Reflections on mifcarriages
of conduct, and miftakes in opinion,
fink it deep into the mind; efpecially
if thofe mifcarriages and miftakes have
been a caufe of pain—when we fmart
for our folly we remember it.

Few people look into their own
hearts, or think of their tempers,
though they feverely cenfure others,
on whofe fide they fay the fault always
lies. Now I am apt to believe, that
there

there is not a temper in the world which does not need correction, and of courfe attention. Thofe who are termed good-humored, are frequently giddy, indolent, and infenfible; yet becaufe the fociety they mix with appear feldom difpleafed with a perfon who does not conteft, and will laugh off an affront, they imagine themfelves pleafing, when they are only not difagreeable. Warm tempers are too eafily irritated. The one requires a fpur, the other a rein. Health of mind, as well as body, muft in general be obtained by patient fubmiffion to felf-denial, and difagreeable operations.

F If

If the prefence of the Deity be inculcated and dwelt on till an habitual reverence is eftablifhed in the mind, it will check the fallies of anger and fneers of peevifhnefs, which corrode our peace, and render us wretched, without any claim to pity.

The wifdom of the Almighty has fo ordered things, that one caufe produces many effects. While we are looking into another's mind, and forming their temper, we are infenfibly correcting our own; and every act of benevolence which we exert to our fellow-creatures, does ourfelves the moft effential fervices. Active virtue

fits

fits us for the fociety of more exalted beings. Our philanthrophy is a proof, we are told, that we are capable of loving our Creator. Indeed this divine love, or charity, appears to me the principal trait that remains of the illuf-trious image of the Deity, which was originally ftampt on the foul, and which is to be renewed. Exalted views will raife the mind above trifling cares, and the many little weakneffes, which make us a torment to ourfelves and others. Our temper will gradu-ally improve, and vanity, which " the creature is made fubject to," has not an entire dominion.

F 2 But

But I have digreffed. A judicious parent can only manage a child in this important article; and example will beft enforce precept.

Be careful, however, not to make hypocrites; fmothered flames will blaze out with more violence for having been kept down. Expect not to do all yourfelf; experience muft enable the child to affift you; you can only lay the foundation, or prevent bad propenfities from fettling into habits.

Un-

Unfortunate Situation of Females, Fashionably Educated, and Left Without a Fortune.

I Have hitherto only fpoken of thofe females, who will have a provifion made for them by their parents. But many who have been well, or at leaft fafhionably educated, are left without a fortune, and if they are not entirely devoid of delicacy, they muft frequently remain fingle.

Few are the modes of earning a fubfiftence, and thofe very humiliating. Perhaps to be an humble companion to fome rich old coufin, or what is ftill

worfe,

worfe, to live with ftrangers, who are fo intolerably tyrannical, that none of their own relations can bear to live with them, though they fhould even expect a fortune in reverfion. It is impoffible to enumerate the many hours of anguifh fuch a perfon muft fpend. Above the fervants, yet confidered by them as a fpy, and ever reminded of her inferiority when in ᴇconverfation with the fuperiors. If fhe cannot condefcend to mean flattery, fhe has not a chance of being a favorite; and fhould any of the vifitors take notice of her, and fhe for a moment forget her fubordinate ftate, fhe is fure to be reminded of it.

Pain-

Painfully fenfible of unkindnefs, fhe is alive to every thing, and many far-cafms reach her, which were perhaps directed another way. She is alone, fhut out from equality and confidence, and the concealed anxiety impairs her conftitution ; for fhe muft wear a cheerful face, or be difmiffed. The being dependant on the caprice of a fellow-creature, though certainly very neceffary in this ftate of difcipline, is yet a very bitter corrective, which we would fain fhrink from.

A teacher at a fchool is only a kind of upper fervant, who has more work than the menial ones.

F 4 A go-

A governess to young ladies is equally disagreeable. It is ten to one if they meet with a reasonable mother; and if she is not so, she will be continually finding fault to prove she is not ignorant, and be displeased if her pupils do not improve, but angry if the proper methods are taken to make them do so. The children treat them with disrespect, and often with insolence. In the mean time life glides away, and the spirits with it; " and when youth and genial years are flown," they have nothing to subsist on; or, perhaps, on some extraordinary occasion, some small allowance may be made for them, which is thought a great charity.

The

The few trades which are left, are now gradually falling into the hands of the men, and certainly they are not very refpectable.

It is hard for a perfon who has a relifh for polifhed fociety, to herd with the vulgar, or to condefcend to mix with her former equals when fhe is confidered in a different light. What unwelcome heart-breaking knowledge is then poured in on her! I mean a view of the felfifhnefs and depravity of the world; for every other acquirement is a fource of pleafure, though they may occafion temporary inconveniences. How cutting is the con-

tempt

tempt fhe meets with!—A young mind looks round for love and friendfhip; but love and friendfhip fly from poverty: expect them not if you are poor! The mind muft then fink into meannefs, and accommodate itfelf to its new ftate, or dare to be unhappy. Yet I think no reflecting perfon would give up the experience and improvement they have gained, to have avoided the misfortunes; on the contrary, they are thankfully ranked amongft the choiceft bleffings of life, when we are not under their immediate preffure.

How earneftly does a mind full of fenfibility look for difinterefted friendfhip,

a

ship, and long to meet with good un-
alloyed. When fortune smiles they
hug the dear delusion; but dream not
that it is one. The painted cloud dif-
appears suddenly, the scene is changed, and what an aching void is left in
the heart! a void which only religion
can fill up—and how few seek this
internal comfort!

A woman, who has beauty without
sentiment, is in great danger of being
seduced; and if she has any, cannot
guard herself from painful mortifica-
tions. It is very disagreeable to keep
up a continual reserve with men she
has been formerly familiar with; yet

if

if she places confidence, it is ten to one but she is deceived. Few men seriously think of marrying an inferior; and if they have honor enough not to take advantage of the artless tendernefs of a woman who loves, and thinks not of the difference of rank, they do not undeceive her until she has anticipated happinefs, which, contrasted with her dependant situation, appears delightful. The disappointment is severe; and the heart receives a wound which does not easily admit of a compleat cure, as the good that is missed is not valued according to its real worth: for fancy drew the picture, and grief delights to create food to feed on.

If

If what I have written should be read by parents, who are now going on in thoughtlefs extravagance, and anxious only that their daughters may be *genteelly educated*, let them confider to what forrows they expofe them ; for I have not over-coloured the picture.

Though I warn parents to guard againft leaving their daughters to en-counter fo much mifery ; yet if a young woman falls into it, fhe ought not to be difcontented. Good muft ulti-mately arife from every thing, to thofe who look beyond this infancy of their being ; and here the comfort of a good confcience is our only ftable fupport. The main bufinefs of our lives is to
learn

learn to be virtuous; and He who is training us up for immortal blifs, knows beſt what trials will contribute to make us ſo; and our reſignation and improvement will render us reſpeſtable to ourſelves, and to that Being, whoſe approbation is of more value than life itſelf.   It is true, tribulation produces anguiſh, and we would fain avoid the bitter cup, though convinced its effeſts would be the moſt ſalutary.   The Almighty is then the kind parent, who chaſtens and educates, and indulges us not when it would tend to our hurt. He is compaſſion itſelf, and never wounds but to heal, when the ends of correſtion are anſwered.

LOVE.

L O V E.

I THINK there is not a fubject that admits fo little of reafoning on as love; nor can rules be laid down that will not appear to lean too much one way or the other. Circumftances muft, in a great meafure, govern the conduct in this particular; yet who can be a judge in their own cafe? Perhaps, before they begin to confider the matter, they fee through the medium of paffion, and its fuggeftions are often miftaken for thofe of reafon. We can no other way account for the abfurd matches we every day have an opportunity of obferving; for in this

refpect,

refpect, even the moft fenfible men and women err. A variety of caufes will occafion an attachment; an endeavour to fupplant another, or being by fome accident confined to the fociety of one perfon. Many have found themfelves entangled in an affair of honor, who only meant to fill up the heavy hours in an amufing way, or raife jealoufy in fome other bofom.

It is a difficult tafk to write on a fubject when our own paffions are likely to blind us. Hurried away by our feelings, we are apt to fet thofe things down as general maxims, which only our partial experience gives rife to.

to. Though it is not eafy to fay how a perfon fhould act under the immediate influence of paffion, yet they certainly have no excufe who are actuated only by vanity, and deceive by an equivocal behaviour in order to gratify it. There are quite as many male coquets as female, and they are far more pernicious pefts to fociety, as their fphere of action is larger, and they are lefs expofed to the cenfure of the world. A fmothered figh, downcaft look, and the many other little arts which are played off, may give extreme pain to a fincere, artlefs woman, though fhe cannot refent, or complain

G   of

of, the injury. This kind of trifling, I think, much more inexcufable than inconftancy; and why it is fo, appears fo obvious, I need not point it out.

People of fenfe and reflection are moft apt to have violent and conftant paffions, and to be preyed on by them. Neither can they, for the fake of prefent pleafure, bear to act in fuch a manner, as that the retrofpect fhould fill them with confufion and regret. Perhaps a delicate mind is not fufceptible of a greater degree of mifery, putting guilt out of the queftion, than what muft arife from the confcioufnefs

of

of loving a perſon whom their reaſon does not approve. This, I am perſuaded, has often been the caſe ; and the paſſion muſt either be rooted out, or the continual allowances and excuſes that are made will hurt the mind, and leſſen the reſpect for virtue. Love, unſupported by eſteem, muſt ſoon expire, or lead to depravity ; as, on the contrary, when a worthy perſon is the object, it is the greateſt incentive to improvement, and has the beſt effect on the manners and temper. We ſhould always try to fix in our minds the rational grounds we have for loving a perſon, that we may be able to recollect them when we feel diſguſt or re-

ſent-

fentment; we fhould then habitually
practife forbearance, and the many
petty difputes which interrupt domeftic
peace would be avoided. A woman
cannot reafonably be unhappy, if fhe
is attached to a man of fenfe and
goodnefs, though he may not be all
fhe could wifh.

I am very far from thinking love
irrefiftible, and not to be conquered.
" If weak women go aftray," it is
they, and not the ftars, that are to be
blamed. A refolute endeavour will
almoft always overcome difficulties.
I. knew a woman very early in life
warmly attached to an agreeable man,

2   yet

yet fhe faw his faults ; his principles
were unfixed, and his prodigal turn
would have obliged her to have reftrained every benevolent emotion of
her heart. She exerted her influence
to improve him, but in vain did fhe
for years try to do it. Convinced of
the impoffibility, fhe determined not to
marry him, though fhe was forced to
encounter poverty and its attendants.

It is too univerfal a maxim with
novelifts, that love is felt but once ;
though it appears to me, that the heart
which is capable of receiving an im-
preffion at all, and can diftinguifh, will
turn to a new obje&t when the firft is

found unworthy. I am convinced it is
practicable, when a refpect for goodnefs has the firft place in the mind,
and notions of perfection are not af-
fixed to conftancy. Many ladies are
delicately miferable, and imagine that
they are lamenting the lofs of a lover,
when they are full of felf-applaufe, and
reflections on their own fuperior refinement. Painful feelings are pro-
longed beyond their natural courfe,
to gratify our defire of appearing he-
roines, and we deceive ourfelves as
well as others. When any fudden ftroke
of fate deprives us of thofe we love,
we may not readily get the better of
the blow; but when we find we have

been led aftray by our paffions, and
that it was our own imaginations
which gave the high colouring to the
picture, we may be certain time will
drive it out of our minds. For we
cannot often think of our folly without being difpleafed with ourfelves,
and fuch reflections are quickly ba-
nifhed. Habit and duty will co-operate, and religion may overcome what
reafon has in vain combated with;
but refinement and romance are often
confounded, and fenfibility, which occafions this kind of inconftancy, is
fuppofed to have the contrary effect.

G 4 No-

Nothing can more tend to deftroy peace of mind, than platonic attachments. They are begun in falfe refinement, and frequently end in forrow, if not in guilt. The two extremes often meet, and virtue carried to excefs will fometimes lead to the oppofite vice. Not that I mean to infinuate that there is no fuch thing as friendfhip between perfons of different fexes; I am convinced of the contrary. I only mean to obferve, that if a woman's heart is difengaged, fhe fhould not give way to a pleafing delufion, and imagine fhe will be fatisfied with the friendfhip of a man fhe admires, and prefers to the reft of the world.

The

The heart is very treacherous, and if we do not guard its firſt emotions, we ſhall not afterwards be able to prevent its ſighing for impoſſibilities. If there are any inſuperable bars to an union in the common way, try to diſmiſs the dangerous tenderneſs, or it will undermine your comfort, and betray you into many errors. To attempt to raiſe ourſelves above human beings is ridiculous; we cannot extirpate our paſſions, nor is it neceſſary that we ſhould, though it may be wiſe ſometimes not to ſtray too near a precipice, leſt we fall over before we are aware. We cannot avoid much vexation and ſorrow, if we are ever ſo prudent; it is then

the

the part of wisdom to enjoy those gleams of sunshine which do not endanger our innocence, or lead to repentance. Love gilds all the prospects of life, and though it cannot always exclude apathy, it makes many cares appear trifling. Dean Swift hated the world, and only loved particular persons; yet pride rivalled them. A foolish wish of rising superior to the common wants and desires of the human species made him singular, but not respectable. He sacrificed an amiable woman to his caprice, and made those shun his company who would have been entertained and improved by his conversation, had he loved any

one

one as well as himfelf. Univerfal benevolence is the firft duty, and we
fhould be careful not to let any paffion fo engrofs our thoughts, as to prevent our practifing it. After all the
dreams of rapture, earthly pleafures
will not fill the mind, or fupport it
when they have not the fanction of
reafon, or are too much depended on.
The tumult of paffion will fubfide,
and even the pangs of difappointment ceafe to be felt. But for the
wicked there is a worm that never
dies—a guilty confcience. While that
calm fatisfaction which refignation
produces, which cannot be defcribed,

but

but may be attained, in fome degree, by thofe who try to keep in the ftrait, though thorny path which leads to blifs, fhall fanctify the forrows, and dignify the character of virtue.

MATRI-

MATRIMONY.

EARLY marriages are, in my opinion, a ſtop to improvement. If we were born only " to draw nutrition, propagate and rot," the ſooner the end of creation was anſwered the better; but as women are here allowed to have ſouls, the ſoul ought to be attended to. In youth a woman endeavours to pleaſe the other ſex, in order, generally ſpeaking, to get married, and this endeavour calls forth all her powers. If ſhe has had a tolerable education, the foundation only is laid, for the mind does not ſoon arrive at maturity, and ſhould not be en-
groſſed

groffed by domeftic cares before any habits are fixed. The paffions alfo have too much influence over the judgment to fuffer it to direct her in this moft important affair; and many women, I am perfuaded, marry a man before they are twenty, whom they would have rejected fome years after. Very frequently, when the education has been neglected, the mind improves itfelf, if it has leifure for reflection, and experience to reflect on; but how can this happen when they are forced to act before they have had time to think, or find that they are unhappily married? Nay, fhould they be fo fortunate as to get a good hufband, they

will

will not fet a proper value on him; he will be found much inferior to the lovers defcribed in novels, and their want of knowledge makes them frequently difgufted with the man, when the fault is in human nature.

When a woman's mind has gained fome ftrength, fhe will in all probability pay more attention to her actions than a girl can be expected to do; and if fhe thinks ferioufly, fhe will chufe for a companion a man of principle; and this perhaps young people do not fufficiently attend to, or fee the neceffity of doing. A woman of feeling muft be very much hurt if fhe

is

is obliged to keep her children out of their father's company, that their morals may not be injured by his converfation ; and befides, the whole arduous tafk of education devolves on her, and in fuch a cafe it is not very practicable. Attention to the education of children muft be irkfome, when life appears to have fo many charms, and its pleafures are not found fallacious. Many are but juft returned from a boarding-fchool, when they are placed at the head of a family, and how fit they are to manage it, I leave the judicious to judge. Can they improve a child's underftanding, when they are fcarcely out of the ftate of childhood themfelves ?

Dignity

Dignity of manners, too, and proper reserve are often wanting. The conftant attendant on too much familiarity is contempt. Women are often before marriage prudifh, and afterwards they think they may innocently give way to fondnefs, and overwhelm the poor man with it. They think they have a legal right to his affections, and grow remifs in their endeavours to pleafe. There are a thoufand name-lefs decencies which good fenfe gives rife to, and artlefs proofs of regard which flow from the heart, and will reach it, if it is not depraved. It has ever occurred to me, that is was fuf-ficient for a woman to receive careffes,

H   and

and not beftow them. She ought to diftinguifh between fondnefs and tendernefs. The latter is the fweeteft cordial of life; but, like all other cordials, fhould be referved for particular occafions; to exhilarate the fpirits, when depreffed by ficknefs, or loft in forrow. Senfibility will beft inftruct. Some delicacies can never be pointed out or defcribed, though they fink deep into the heart, and render the hours of diftrefs fupportable.

A woman fhould have fo proper a pride, as not eafily to forget a deliberate affront; though fhe muft not too haftily refent any little coolnefs. We

3

We cannot always feel alike, and all are fubject to changes of temper without an adequate caufe.

Reafon muft often be called in to fill up the vacuums of life; but too many of our fex fuffer theirs to lie dormant. A little ridicule and fmart turn of expreffion, often confutes without convincing; and tricks are played off to raife tendernefs, even while they are forfeiting efteem.

Women are faid to be the weaker veffel, and many are the miferies which this weaknefs brings on them. Men have in fome refpects very much the ad-

H 2   vantage.

vantage. If they have a tolerable understanding, it has a chance to be cultivated. They are forced to fee human nature as it is, and are not left to dwell on the pictures of their own imaginations. Nothing, I am fure, calls forth the faculties fo much as the being obliged to ftruggle with the world; and this is not a woman's province in a married ftate. Her fphere of action is not large, and if fhe is not taught to look into her own heart, how trivial are her occupations and purfuits! What little arts engrofs and narrow her mind! " Cunning fills up the mighty void of fenfe;" and cares, which do not improve the heart or un

derftand

derftanding, take up her attention. Of courfe, fhe falls a prey to childifh anger, and filly capricious humors, which render her rather infignificant than vicious.

In a comfortable fituation, a culti-vated mind is neceffary to render a woman contented; and in a miferable one, it is her only confolation. A fen-fible, delicate woman, who by fome ftrange accident, or miftake, is joined to a fool or a brute, muft be wretched beyond all names of wretchednefs, if her views are confined to the prefent fcene. Of what importance, then, is intellectual improvement, when our

H 3   com-

comfort here, and happinefs hereafter, depends upon it.

Principles of religion fhould be fix-ed, and the mind not left to fluctuate in the time of diftrefs, when it can re-ceive fuccour from no other quarter. The conviction that every thing is working for our good will fcarcely produce refignation, when we are de-prived of our deareft hopes. How they can be fatisfied, who have not this conviction, I cannot conceive ; I rather think they will turn to fome worldly fupport, and fall into folly, if not vice. For a little refinement only leads a woman into the wilds of ro-mance,

mance, if she is not religious; nay, more, there is no true sentiment without it, nor perhaps any other effectual check to the passions.

DE-

DESULTORY THOUGHTS.

AS every kind of domeftic concern and family bufinefs is properly a woman's province, to enable her to difcharge her duty fhe fhould ftudy the different branches of it. Nothing is more ufeful in a family than a little knowledge of phyfic, fufficient to make the miftrefs of it a judicious nurfe. Many a perfon, who has had a fenfible phyfician to attend them, have been loft for want of the other; for tendernefs, without judgment, fometimes does more harm than good.

The ignorant imagine there is fomething very myfterious in the practice

of

of phyfic. They expect a medicine
to work like a charm, and know nothing of the progrefs and crifis of dif-
orders. The keeping of the patient low
appears cruel, all kind of regimen is
difregarded, and though the fever
rages, they cannot be perfuaded not
to give them inflammatory food.
" How (fay they) can a perfon get well
without nourifhment ?"

The mind, too, fhould be foothed
at the fame time; and indeed, whenever it finks, foothing is, at firft, better
than reafoning. The flackened nerves
are not to be braced by words. When
a mind is worried by care; or oppreffed

by

by forrow, it cannot in a moment
grow tranquil, and attend to the voice
of reafon.

St. Paul fays, " No chaftening for
the prefent feemeth to be joyous ; but
grievous : neverthelefs, afterwards it
yieldeth the peaceable fruits of righte-
oufnefs unto them which are exercifed
thereby." It is plain, from thefe
words of the Apoftle, and from many
other parts of Scripture, that afflictions are neceffary to teach us true
wifdom, and that in fpite of this conviction, men would fain avoid the
bitter draught, though certain that the
drinking of it would be conducive to
the

the purifying of their hearts. He who
made us muſt know what will tend to
our ultimate good ; yet ſtill all this is
grievous, and the heart will throb with
anguiſh when deprived of what it loves,
and the tongue can ſcarcely faulter
out an acquieſcence to the Divine Will,
when it is ſo contrary to our own. Due
allowance ought then to be made for
human infirmities, and the unhappy
ſhould be conſidered as objects of compaſſion, rather than blame. But in a very
different ſtile does conſolatory advice
generally run ; for inſtead of pouring
oil or wine into the wound, it tends
to convince the unfortunate perſons
that they are weak as well as unhappy.

I am

I am apt to imagine, that forrow and
refignation are not incompatible ; and
that though religion cannot make fome
difappointments pleafant, it prevents
our repining, even while we fmart under them. Did our feelings and reafon
always coincide, our paffage through
this world could not juftly be termed
a warfare, and faith would no longer
be a virtue. It is our preferring the
things that are not feen, to thofe which
are, that proves us to be the heirs of
promife.

On the facred word of the Moft
High, we rely with firm affurance,
that the fufferings of the prefent life
will

will work out a far more exceeding
and eternal weight of glory; yet ftill
they are allowed to be afflictions,
which, though temporary, muft ftill
be grievous.

The difference between thofe who
forrow without hope, and thofe who
look up to Heaven, is not that the
one feel more than the other, for they
may be both equally depreffed; but
the latter think of the peaceable fruits
which are to refult from the difcipline, and therefore patiently fubmit.

I have almoft run into a fermon,—
and I fhall not make an apology for it.
                                  What-

Whatever contributes to make us compaffionate and refolute, is of the utmoft confequence; both thefe qualities are neceffary, if we are confined to a fick chamber. Various are the misfortunes of life, and it may be the lot of moft of us to fee death in all its terrors, when it attacks a friend; yet even then we muft exert our friend-fhip, and try to chear the departing fpirit.

THE

THE BENEFITS WHICH ARISE FROM DISAPPOINMENTS.

MOST women, and men too, have no character at all. Juft opinions and virtuous paffions appear by ftarts, and while we are giving way to the love and admiration which thofe qualities raife, they are quite different creatures. It is reflection which forms habits, and fixes principles indelibly on the heart; without it, the mind is like a wreck drifted about by every fquall. The paffion that we think moft of will foon rival all the reft; it is then in our power, this way, to ftrengthen our

good

good difpofitions, and in fome meafure
to eftablifh a character, which will not
depend on every accidental impulfe.
To be convinced of truths, and yet
not to feel or act up to them, is a
common thing. Prefent pleafure drives
all before it, and adverfity is merci-
fully fent to force us to think.

In the fchool of adverfity we learn
knowledge as well as virtue; yet we
lament our hard fate, dwell on our difappointments, and never confider that
our own wayward minds, and incon-
fiftent hearts, require thefe needful
correctives. Medicines are not fent
to perfons in health.

It

It is a well-known remark, that our very wifhes give us not our wifh. I have often thought it might be fet down as a maxim, that the greateft difappointment we can meet with is the gratification of our fondeft wifhes. But truth is fometimes not pleafant; we turn from it, and doat on an illufion; and if we were not in a probationary ftate, we fhould do well to thicken the cloud, rather than difpel it.

There are fome who delight in obferving moral beauty, and their fouls ficken when forced to view crimes and follies which could never hurt them. How numerous are the forrows which

I   reach

reach fuch bofoms! They may truly be called *human creatures*; on every fide they touch their fellow-mortals, and vibrate to the touch. Common humanity points out the important duties of our ftation; but fenfibility (a kind of inftinct, ftrengthened by reflection) can only teach the numberlefs minute things which give pain or pleafure.

A benevolent mind often fuffers more than the object it commiferates, and will bear an inconvenience itfelf to fhelter another from it. It makes allowance for failings though it longs to meet perfection, which it feems formed

formed to adore. The Author of all good continually calls himfelf, a God long-fuffering; and thofe moft refemble him who practife forbearance. Love and compaffion are the moft delightful feelings of the foul, and to exert them to all that breathe is the wifh of the benevolent heart. To ftruggle with ingratitude and felfifhnefs is grating beyond expreffion: and the fenfe we have of our weaknefs, though ufeful, is not pleafant. Thus it is with us, when we look for happinefs, we meet with vexations: and if, now and then, we give way to tendernefs, or any of the amiable paffions, and tafte pleafure, the mind, ftrained beyond its

I 2 ufual

uſual tone, falls into apathy.   And yet
we were made to be happy! But our
paſſions will not contribute much to
our bliſs, till they are under the dominion of reaſon, and till that reaſon
is enlightened and improved.   Then
ſighing will ceaſe, and all tears will be
wiped away by that Being, in whoſe
preſence there is fulneſs of joy.

A perſon of tenderneſs muſt ever
have particular attachments, and ever
be diſappointed; yet ſtill they muſt be
attached, in ſpite of human frailty;
for if the mind is not kept in motion
by either hope or fear, it ſinks into
the dreadful ſtate before-mentioned.

I have

I have very often heard it made a fubject of ridicule, that when a perfon is difappointed in this world, they turn to the next. Nothing can be more natural than the tranfition; and it feems to me the fcheme of Providence, that our finding things unfatisfactory here, fhould force us to think of the better country to which we are going.

ON

ON THE TREATMENT OF SERVANTS.

THE management of fervants is a great part of the employment of a woman's life; and her own temper depends very much on her behaviour to them.

Servants are, in general, ignorant and cunning; we muft confider their charaƈters, if we would treat them properly, and continually praƈtife forbearance. The fame methods we ufe with children may be adopted with regard to them. Aƈt uniformly, and never find fault without a juft caufe;

and

and when there is, be pofitive, but not
angry. A mind that is not too much
engroffed by trifles, will not be difcom-
pofed by every little domeftic difafter;
and a thinking perfon can very readily
make allowance for thofe faults which
arife from want of reflection and education. I have feen the peace of a
whole family difturbed by fome trivial,
crofs accident, and hours fpent in ufe-
lefs upbraidings about fome miftake
which would never have been thought
of, but for the confequences that arofe
from it. An error in judgment or an
accident fhould not be feverely repre-
hended. It is a proof of wifdom to

profit.

profit by experience, and not lament irremediable evils.

A benevolent perfon muſt ever wiſh to ſee thoſe around them comfortable, and try to be the cauſe of that comfort. The wide difference which education makes, I ſhould ſuppoſe, would prevent familiarity in the way of equality; yet kindneſs muſt be ſhewn, if we are defirous that our domeſtics ſhould be attached to our intereſt and perſons. How pleaſing it is to be attended with a ſmile of willingneſs, to be conſulted when they are at a loſs, and looked up to as a friend and benefaċtor when they are in diſtreſs. It

is

is true we may often meet with ingratitude, but it ought not to difcourage us; the refrefhing fhowers of heaven fertilize the fields of the unworthy, as well as the juft. We fhould nurfe them in illnefs, and our fuperior judgment in thofe matters would often alleviate their pains.

Above all, we owe them a good example. The ceremonials of religion, on their account, fhould be attended to; as they always reverence them to a fuperftitious degree, or elfe neglect them. We fhould not fhock the faith of the meaneft fellow-creature; nay more, we fhould comply

with

with their prejudices; for their religious notions are fo over-run with
them, that they are not eafily feparat-
ed; and by trying to pluck up the
tares, we may root up the wheat with
them.

The woman who gives way to caprice and ill-humour in the kitchen,
cannot eafily fmooth her brow when
her hufband returns to his fire-fide;
nay, he may not only fee the wrinkles
of anger, but hear the difputes at
fecond-hand. I heard a Gentleman
fay, it would break any man's heart to
hear his wife argue fuch a cafe. Men
who are employed about things of

confe-

confequence, think thefe affairs more infignificant than they really are; for the warmth with which we engage in any bufinefs increafes its importance, and our not entering into them has the contrary effect.

The behaviour of girls to fervants is generally in extremes; too familiar or haughty. Indeed the one often produces the other, as a check, when the freedoms are troublefome.

We cannot make our fervants wife or good, but we may teach them to be decent and orderly; and order leads to fome degree of morality.

THE

THE OBSERVANCE OF SUNDAY.

THE inftitution of keeping the feventh day holy was wifely or-dered by Providence for two purpofes. To reft the body, and call off the mind from the too eager purfuit of the fhadows of this life, which, I am afraid, often obfcure the profpect of futurity, and fix our thoughts on earth. A refpect for this ordinance is, I am perfuaded, of the utmoft confequence to national religion. The vulgar have fuch a notion of it, that with them, going to church, and being religious, are almoft fynonymous terms. They

are

are fo loft in their fenfes, that if this day did not continually remind them, they would foon forget that there was a God in the world. Some forms are neceffary to fupport vital religion, and without them it would foon languifh, and at laft expire.

It is unfortunate, that this day is either kept with puritanical exactnefs, which renders it very irkfome, or loft in diffipation and thoughtleffnefs. Either way is very prejudicial to the minds of children and fervants, who ought not to be let run wild, nor confined too ftrictly; and, above all, fhould not fee their parents or mafters

indulge

indulge themfelves in things which are generally thought wrong. I am fully perfuaded, that fervants have fuch a notion of card-playing, that where-ever it is practifed of a Sunday their minds are hurt; and the barrier be-tween good and evil in fome meafure broken down. Servants, who are ac-cuftomed to bodily labour, will fall into as laborious pleafures, if they are not gently reftrained, and fome fub-ftitute found out for them.

Such a clofe attention to a family may appear to many very difagree-able; but the path of duty will be found pleafant after fome time; and

the

the paffions being employed this way, will, by degrees, come under the fub- jection of reafon. I mean not to be rigid, the obftructions which arife in the way of our duty, do not ftrike a fpeculatift ; I know, too, that in the moment of action, even a well-difpofed mind is often carried away by the prefent impulfe, and that it requires fome experience to be able to diftin- guifh the dictates of reafon from thofe of paffion. The truth is feldom found out until the tumult is over ; we then wake as from a dream, and when we furvey what we have done, and feel the folly of it, we might call on rea- fon and fay, why fleepeft thou ? Yet
though

though people are led aftray by their paffions, and even relapfe after the moft bitter repentance, they fhould not defpair, but ftill try to regain the right road, and cultivate fuch habits as may affift them.

I never knew much focial virtue to refide in a houfe where the fabbath was grofsly violated.

ON

ON THE MISFORTUNE OF FLUCTUATING PRINCIPLES.

IF we look for any comfort in friend-
ship or fociety, we muft affociate
with thofe who have fixed principles
with refpect to religion; for without
them, repeated experience convinces
me, the moft fhining qualities are un-
ftable, and not to be depended on.

It has often been a matter of fur-
prife to me, that fo few people examine the tenets of the religion they
profefs, or are chriftians through conviction. They have no anchor to reft
on, nor any fixed chart to direct them

K in

in the doubtful voyage of life; how then can they hope to find the " haven of reſt ?" But they think not of it, and cannot be expected to forego preſent advantages. Noble actions muſt ariſe from noble thoughts and views ; when they are confined to this world, they muſt be groveling.

Faith, with reſpect to the promiſe of eternal happineſs, can only enable us to combat with our paſſions, with a chance of victory. There are many who pay no attention to revelation, and more, perhaps, who have not any fixed belief in it. The ſure word of comfort is neglected ; and how people

can

can live without it, I can fcarcely conceive. For as the fun renews the face of nature, and chafes away darknefs from the world, fo does this, ftill greater bleffing, have the fame effect on the mind, and enlightens and cheers it when every thing elfe fails.

A true fenfe of our infirmities is the way to make us chriftians in the moft extenfive fenfe of the word. A mind depreffed with a weight of weakneffes can only find comfort in the promifes of the Gofpel. The affiftance there offered muft raife the humble foul; and the account of the atonement that has been made, gives a rational

K 2 ground

ground for refting in hope until the toil of virtue is over, and faith has nothing to be exercifed on.

It is the fafhion now for young men to be deifts. And many a one has improper books fent adrift in a fea of doubts—of which there is no end. This is not a land of certainty; there is no confining the wandering reafon, and but one clue to prevent its being loft in endlefs refearches. Reafon is indeed the heaven-lighted lamp in man, and may fafely be trufted when not entirely depended on; but when it pretends to difcover what is beyond its ken, it certainly ftretches

the

the line too far, and runs into abfurdity. Some fpeculations are idle and
others hurtful, as they raife pride, and
turn the thoughts to fubjects that
ought to be left unexplored. With
love and awe we fhould think of the
High and Lofty One, that inhabiteth
eternity! and not prefume to fay how
He muft exift who created us. How
unfortunate it is, that man muft fink
into a brute, and not employ his mind,
or elfe, by thinking, grow fo proud,
as often to imagine himfelf a fuperior being! It is not the doubts of
profound thinkers that I here allude
to, but the crude notions which young
men fport away when together, and

fome-

fometimes in the company of young women, to make them wonder at their fuperior wifdom ! There cannot be any thing more dangerous to a mind, not accuftomed to think, than doubts delivered in a ridiculing way. They never go deep enough to folve them, of courfe they ftick by them; and though they might not influence their conduct, if a fear of the world prevents their being guilty of vices, yet their thoughts are not reftrained, and they fhould be obferved diligently, " For out of them are the iffues of life." A nice fenfe of right and wrong ought to be acquired, and then not only great vices will be avoided, but every little meannefs; truth will reign

in

in the inward parts, and mercy will attend her.

I have indeed fo much compaffion for thofe young females who are en- tering into the world without fixed principles, that I would fain perfuade them to examine a little into the matter. For though in the feafon of gaiety they may not feel the want of them, in that of diftrefs where will they fly for fuccour? Even with this fupport, life is a labor of patience—a conflict; and the utmoft we can gain is a fmall portion of peace, a kind of watchful tranquillity, that is liable to continual interruptions.

K 4   " Then

" Then keep each paffion down, however dear;

" Truft me, the tender are the moft fevere.

" Guard, while 'tis thine, thy philofophic eafe,

" And afk no joy but that of virtuous peace;

" That bids defiance to the ftorms of fate:

" High blifs is only for a higher ftate."

THOMSON.

BENE-

BENEVOLENCE.

THIS firft, and moft amiable virtue, is often found in young
perfons that afterwards grow felfifh;
a knowledge of the arts of others, is
an excufe to them for practifing the
fame; and becaufe they have been
deceived once, or have found objects
unworthy of their charity—if any one
appeals to their feelings, the formida-
ble word Impofture inftantly banifhes
the compaffionate emotions, and fi-
lences confcience. I do not mean to
confine the exercife of benevolence to
alms-giving, though it is a very mate-
rial part of it. Faith, hope, and cha-

rity, ought to attend us in our paſſage through this world ; but the two firſt leave us when we die, while the other is to be the conſtant inmate of our breaſt through all eternity. We ought not to ſuffer the heavenly ſpark to be quenched by ſelfiſhneſs ; if we do, how can we expeƈt it to revive, when the ſoul is diſentangled from the body, and ſhould be prepared for the realms of love ? Forbearance and liberality of ſentiment are the virtues of matu- rity. Children ſhould be taught every thing in a poſitive way ; and their own experience can only teach them after- wards to make diſtinƈtions and allow- ances. It is then the inferior part of

bene-

benevolence that comes within their sphere of action, and it should not be suffered to sleep. Some part of the money that is allowed them for pocket-money, they should be encouraged to lay out this way, and the short-lived emotions of pity continually retraced 'till they grow into habits.

I knew a child that would, when very young, sit down and cry if it met a poor person, after it had laid out its money in cakes; this occurred once or twice, and the tears were shed with additional distress every time; till at last it resisted the temptation, and saved the money.

I think

I think it a very good method for girls to have a certain allowance for cloaths. A mother can eafily, without feeming to do it, obferve how they fpend it, and direct them accordingly. By thefe means they would learn the value of money, and be obliged to contrive. This would be a practical leffon of œconomy fuperior to all the theories that could be thought of. The having a fixed ftipend, too, would enable them to be charitable, in the true fenfe of the word, as they would then give their own ; and by denying themfelves little ornaments, and doing their own work, they might increafe the fum appropriated to charitable purpofes.

A lively

A lively principle of this kind would alſo overcome indolence; for I have known people waſteful and penurious at the ſame time; but the waſteful-neſs was to ſpare themſelves trouble, and others only felt the effects of their penury, to make the balance even.

Women too often confine their love and charity to their own families. They fix not in their minds the prece-dency of moral obligations, or make their feelings give way to duty. Good-will to all the human race ſhould dwell in our boſoms, nor ſhould love to in-dividuals induce us to violate this firſt of duties, or make us ſacrifice the in-tereſt

tereft of any fellow-creature, to pro-
mote that of another, whom we happen
to be more partial to. A parent, under
-diftreffed circumftances, fhould be fup-
ported, even though it fhould prevent
our faving a fortune for a child; nay
more, fhould they be both in diftrefs
at the fame time, the prior obligation
fhould be firft difcharged.

Under this head may be included
the treatment of animals. Over them
many children tyrannize with impu-
nity; and find amufement in tormenting,
or wantonly killing, any infect that
comes in their way, though it does
them no injury. I am perfuaded, if
they

they were told ſtories of them, and led to take an intereſt in their welfare and occupations, they would be tender to them ; as it is, they think man the only thing of conſequence in the creation. I once prevented a girl's killing ants, for ſport, by adapting Mr. Addiſon's account of them to her underſtanding. Ever after ſhe was careful not to tread on them, left ſhe ſhould diſtreſs the whole community.

Stories of inſects and animals are the firſt that ſhould rouſe the childiſh paſſions, and exerciſe humanity ; and then they will riſe to man, and from him to his Maker.

CARD-

CARD-PLAYING.

CARD-playing is now the conftant amufement, I may fay employ-ment, of young and old, in genteel life. After all the fatigue of the toilet, blooming girls are fet down to card-tables, and the moft unpleafing paf-fions called forth. Avarice does not wait for grey hairs and wrinkles, but marks a countenance where the loves and graces ought to revel. The hours that fhould be fpent in improving the mind, or in innocent mirth, are thus thrown away ; and if the ftake is not confiderable enough to roufe the paf-fions, loft in infipidity, and a habit ac-quired

quired which may lead to ſerious miſ-
chief. Not to talk of gaming, many
people play for more than they can
well afford to loſe, and this ſours their
temper. Cards are the univerſal refuge
to which the idle and the ignorant re-
ſort, to paſs life away, and to keep their
inactive ſouls awake, by the tumult of
hope and fear.

" Unknown to them, when ſenſual plea͟
    " ſures cloy,
" To fill the languid pauſe with finer joy;
" Unknown thoſe powers that raiſe the ſoul
    " to flame,
" Catch every nerve, and vibrate through
    " the frame."

And, of courſe, this is their favourite
amuſement. Silent, ſtupid attention

appears neceſſary; and too frequently little arts are practiſed which debaſe the character, and at beſt give it a trifling turn. Certainly nothing can be more abſurd than permitting girls to acquire a fondneſs for cards. In youth the imagination is lively, and novelty gives charms to every ſcene; pleaſure almoſt obtrudes itſelf, and the pliable mind and warm affections are eaſily wrought on. They want not thoſe reſources, which even reſpectable and ſenſible perſons ſometimes find neceſſary, when they ſee life, as it is unſatisfactory, and cannot anticipate pleaſures, which they know will fade when nearly viewed. Youth

I

is the feafon of activity, and fhould not be loft in liftleffnefs. Knowledge ought to be acquired, a laudable ambition encouraged; and even the errors of paffion may produce ufeful experience, expand the faculties, and teach them to know their own hearts. The moft fhining abilities, and the moft amiable difpofitions of the mind, require culture, and a proper fituation, not only to ripen and improve them, but to guard them againft the perverfions of vice, and the contagious influence of bad examples.

L 2 THE

THE THEATRE.

THE amusements which this place afford are generally supposed the most rational, and are really so to a cultivated mind; yet one that is not quite formed may learn affectation at the theatre. Many of our admired tragedies are too full of declamation, and a false display of the passions. A heroine is often made to grieve ten or twenty years, and yet the unabated sorrow has not given her cheeks a pallid hue; she still inspires the most violent passion in every beholder, and her own yields not to time. The prominent features of a passion are easily

4   copied,

copied, while the more delicate touches are overlooked. That ftart of Cordelia's, when her father fays, " I think that Lady is my daughter," has affected me beyond meafure, when I could unmoved hear Califta defcribe the cave in which fhe would live " Until her tears had wafhed her guilt away."

The principal characters are too frequently made to rife above human nature, or fink below it; and this occafions many falfe conclufions. The chief ufe of dramatic performances fhould be to teach us to difcriminate characters; but if we reft in feparat-

L 3   ing

ing the good from the bad, we are very fuperficial obfervers. May I venture a conjecture?—I cannot help thinking, that every human creature has fome fpark of goodnefs, which their long-fuffering and benevolent Father gives them an opportunity of improving, though they may perverfely fmother it before they ceafe to breathe.

Death is treated in too flight a manner; and fought, when difappointments occur, with a degree of impatience, which proves that the main end of life has not been confidered. That fearful punifhment of fin, and convulfion of nature, is too often expofed poſed to public view. Until very lately I never had the courage even to look at a perſon dying on the ſtage. The hour of death is not the time for the diſplay of paſſions ; nor do I think it natural it ſhould: the mind is then dreadfully diſturbed, and the trifling ſorrows of this world not thought of. The deaths on the ſtage, in ſpite of the boaſted ſenſibility of the age, ſeem to have much the ſame effect on a polite audience, as the execution of malefactors has on the mob that follow them to Tyburn.

The worſt ſpecies of immorality is inculcated, and life (which is to determine the fate of eternity) thrown away when

I 4 a king-a kingdom or miftrefs is loft. Patience and fubmiffion to the will of Heaven, and thofe virtues which render us ufeful to fociety, are not brought forward to view; nor can they occafion thofe furprifing turns of fortune which moft delight vulgar minds. The almoft imperceptible progrefs of the paffions, which Shakefpeare has fo finely delineated, are not fufficiently obferved, though the ftart of the actor is applauded. Few tragedies, I think, will pleafe a perfon of difcernment, and their fenfibility is fure to be hurt.

Young perfons, who are happily fituated, do well to enter into fictitious

tious diftrefs ; and if they have any
judicious perfon to direct their judgment, it may be improved while their
hearts are melted. Yet I would not
have them confine their compaffion to
the diftreffes occafioned by love ; and
perhaps their feelings might more pro-
fitably be roufed, if they were to fee
fometimes the complicated mifery of
ficknefs and poverty, and weep for the
beggar inftead of the king.

Comedy is not now fo cenfurable as
it was fome years ago ; and a chafte
ear is not often fhocked with inde-
cencies. When follies are pointed
out, and vanity ridiculed, it may be
very

very improving; and perhaps the stage is the only place where ridicule is useful.

What I have said is certainly only applicable to those who go to see the play, and not to shew themselves and waste time. The most insignificant amusement will afford instruction to thinking minds, and the most rational will be lost on a vacant one.

Remarks on the actors are frequently very tiresome. It is a fashionable topic, and a thread-bare one; it requires great abilities, and a knowledge of nature, to be a competent

petent judge; and thofe who do not enter into the fpirit of the author, are not qualified to converfe with confidence on the fubject.

PUBLIC

PUBLIC PLACES.

UNDER this head I rank all thofe places, which are open to an indifcriminate refort of company. There feems at prefent fuch a rage for pleafure, that when adverfity does not call home the thoughts, the whole day is moftly fpent in preparations and plans, or in actual diffipation. Solitude appears infupportable, and domeftic comfort ftupid. And though the amufements may not always be relifhed, the mind is fo enervated it cannot exert itfelf to find out any other fubftitute. An immoderate fondnefs for drefs is acquired, and many fafhion-

able

able females fpend half the night in going from one place to another to difplay their finery, repeat commonplace compliments, and raife envy,in their acquaintance whom they endeavour to outfhine. Women, who are engaged in thofe fcenes, muft fpend more time in drefs than they ought to do, and it will occupy their thoughts when they fhould be better employed.

In the fine Lady how few traits do we obferve of thofe affections which dignify human nature! If fhe has any maternal tendernefs, it is of a childifh kind. We cannot be too careful not to verge on this character; though
fhe

she lives many years she is still a child in understanding, and of so little use to society, that her death would scarcely be observed.

Dissipation leads to poverty, which cannot be patiently borne by those who have lived on the vain applause of others, on account of outward advantages; these were the things they imagined of most consequence, and of course they are tormented with false shame, when by a reverse of fortune they are deprived of them.

A young innocent girl, when she first enters into gay scenes, finds her
spirits

spirits so raised by them, that she would often be lost in delight, if she was not checked by observing the behaviour of a class of females who attend those places. What a painful train of reflections do then arise in the mind, and convictions of the vice and folly of the world are prematurely forced on it. It is no longer a paradise, for innocence is not there; the taint of vice poisons every enjoyment, and affectation, though despised, is very contagious. If these reflections do not occur, languor follows the extraordinary exertions, and weak minds fall a prey to imaginary distress, to banish which they are obliged to take as a remedy what produced the disease.

We

We talk of amufements unbending the mind; fo they ought; yet even in the hours of relaxation we are acquiring habits. A mind accuftomed to obferve can never be quite idle, and will catch improvement on all occafions. Our purfuits and pleafures fhould have the fame tendency, and every thing concur to prepare us for a ftate of purity and happinefs. There vice and folly will not poifon our pleafures; our faculties will expand, and not miftake their objects; and we fhall no longer " fee as through a " glafs darkly, but know, even as we " are known."

F I N I S.

ALSO AVAILABLE FROM THOEMMES PRESS

For Her Own Good – A Series of Conduct Books

Cœlebs in Search of a Wife
Hannah More
With a new introduction by Mary Waldron
ISBN 1 85506 383 2 : 288pp : 1808–9 edition : £14.75

Female Replies to Swetnam the Woman-Hater
Various
With a new introduction by Charles Butler
ISBN 1 85506 379 4 : 336pp : 1615–20 edition : £15.75

A Complete Collection of Genteel and Ingenious Conversation
Jonathan Swift
With a new introduction by the Rt Hon. Michael Foot
ISBN 1 85506 380 8 : 224pp : 1755 edition : £13.75

Thoughts on the Education of Daughters
Mary Wollstonecraft
With a new introduction by Janet Todd
ISBN 1 85506 381 6 : 192pp : 1787 edition : £13.75

The Young Lady's Pocket Library, or Parental Monitor
Various
With a new introduction by Vivien Jones
ISBN 1 85506 382 4 : 352pp : 1790 edition : £15.75

Also available as a 5 volume set : ISBN 1 85506 378 6
Special Set Price: £65.00

Her Write His Name

Old Kensington *and* The Story of Elizabeth
Anne Isabella Thackeray
With a new introduction by Esther Schwartz-McKinzie
ISBN 1 85506 388 3 : 496pp : 1873 & 1876 editions : £17.75

Shells from the Sands of Time
Rosina Bulwer Lytton
With a new introduction by Marie Mulvey Roberts
ISBN 1 85506 386 7 : 272pp : 1876 edition : £14.75

Platonics
Ethel Arnold
With a new introduction by Phyllis Wachter
ISBN 1 85506 389 1 : 160pp : 1894 edition : £13.75

The Continental Journals 1798-1820
Dorothy Wordsworth
With a new introduction by Helen Boden
ISBN 1 85506 385 9 : 472pp : New edition : £17.75

Her Life in Letters
Alice James
Edited with a new introduction by Linda Anderson
ISBN 1 85506 387 5 : 320pp : New : £15.75

Also available as a 5 volume set : ISBN 1 8556 384 0
Special set price : £70.00

Subversive Women

The Art of Ingeniously Tormenting
Jane Collier
With a new introduction by Judith Hawley
ISBN 1 8556 246 1 : 292pp : 1757 edition : £14.75

Appeal of One Half the Human Race, Women, Against the Pretensions of the Other Half, Men, to Retain them in Political, and thence in Civil and Domestic, Slavery
William Thompson and Anna Wheeler
With a new introduction by the Rt Hon. Michael Foot and Marie Mulvey Roberts
ISBN 1 85506 247 X : 256pp : 1825 edition : £14.75

A Blighted Life: A True Story
Rosina Bulwer Lytton
With a new introduction by Marie Mulvey Roberts
ISBN 1 85506 248 8 : 178pp : 1880 edition : £10.75

The Beth Book
Sarah Grand
With a new introduction by Sally Mitchell
ISBN 1 85506 249 6 : 560pp : 1897 edition : £18.75

The Journal of a Feminist
Elsie Clews Parsons
With a new introduction and notes by Margaret C. Jones
ISBN 1 85506 250 X : 142pp : New edition : £12.75

Also available as a 5 volume set : ISBN 1 85506 261 5
Special set price : £65.00

JANET TODD
is a professor of English at the University of East
Anglia, Norwich. She was formerly a professor of
English at Rutgers University in New Jersey and a
Fellow of Sidney Sussex College, Cambridge. She has
written many books on feminist criticism and women
writers in the Restoration and eighteenth century, her
most recent ones being *Feminist Literary History*
(Polity, 1988), *The Sign of Angellica: woman, writing
and fiction 1660-1800* (Virago, 1990), and *Gender, Art
and Death* (Polity, 1993). She has brought out works
of Eliza Fenwick, Charlotte Smith and Helen Maria
Williams and, with Marilyn Butler, edited the complete
works of Mary Wollstonecraft. She is currently editing
the complete works of Aphra Behn and writing her
biography.

Marie Mulvey Roberts is a Senior Lecturer in literary
studies at the University of the West of England and is
the author of *British Poets and Secret Societies* (1986),
and *Gothic Immortals* (1990). From 1994 she has been
the co-editor of a Journal: 'Women's Writing; the
Elizabethan to the Victorian Period', and the General
Editor for three series: *Subversive Women, For Her Own
Good*, and *Her Write His Name*. The volumes she has
co-edited include: *Sources of British Feminism* (1993),
Perspectives on the History of British Feminism (1994),
Controversies in the History of British Feminism (1995)
and *Literature and Medicine during the Eighteenth
Century* (1993). Among her single edited books are,
Out of the Night: Writings from Death Row (1994), and
editions of Rosina Bulwer Lytton's *A Blighted Life*
(1994) and *Shells from the Sands of Time* (1995).

COVER ILLUSTRATION
An Establishment for Young Ladies *by F. Burney*
reproduced by permission of the Victoria and Albert
Museum.
Cover designed by Dan Broughton